Tools for Spiritual Freedom

Contents

Published by Alarias Press, LLC

ISBN: 979-8-9869679-1-2

Have you struggled with rejection, fear, or a broken heart?

Author Carolyn Rice struggled with all of these and more. There were times she felt alone and isolated, like the only one who understood at all was God.

God Sees Your Tears is a collection of prayers calling out to God for help with discouragement, anger, shame, bad memories and more. Each prayer comes with a Scripture to find comfort from God's Word.

You don't have to feel alone anymore.

Subscribe to Carolyn's newsletter and download your free gift at CarolynsBooks.com today.

Introduction

I stood in church that Christmas Eve, with a lit candle in my hand. The lights dimmed, and we were all met with the beautiful sight of our candles illuminating the room.

During that moment, a thought came to mind.

The Bible says we are the light of the world (See Matthew 5:14), but there are candles that have lost their light, the enemy coming at them in different ways until they quit.

Dear sister, you are the light of the world, and the enemy of your soul wants to blow your candle out, so that your light does not shine.

He does it through people who are being used as his tools, held captive to do his will (See 2 Timothy 2:26). He does it through circumstances, negative thoughts, and bringing to your mind the question, "Did God really say? Are His promises true for me?" as if you are somehow less than everyone else.

The enemy of your soul wants you to give up hope, give in to discouragement, throw in the towel, and think that God has abandoned you or won't come through on your behalf.

Whether we like it or not, we find ourselves in the middle of spiritual warfare, when we are simply trying to live our lives for Jesus.

Which is where *this* Bible study comes in.

Each day you will find a tool that you can use to stand against the enemy and his ploys to take out your light. By the end of this study, you will be equipped to stand firm and let your light shine brightly in this dark world.

You will be stronger and equipped for the battles you face in this life.

Feel free to do this study individually or as a group, using the reflection questions to discuss the Scriptures covered that day. The study can be done in thirty days, or in 6 weeks time if you work through it at the rate of 5 days per week.

My prayer for you, however you implement the study, is that you will come away equipped with powerful prayers and tools to stand your ground, and after you have done everything, to stand (See Ephesians 6:13).

In His Love,

Carolyn Rice

Acknowledgements

To my husband Lyle. Without your support, encouragement and prayers, this book would not have been written.

To my wonderful prayer team who has interceded for every part of this book, from beginning to end. I am so very thankful for your prayers over me, this book, my podcast and YouTube channel. From the bottom of my heart, I am so incredibly thankful for each one of you.

To my Heavenly Father. Thank you for making yourself real to me.

Rejecting Rejection

Read: Ephesians 1:1-5

Not chosen.

That is how I felt.

My past had dictated to my heart that my worth and value must be nothing.

One day, I sat in my chair, my Bible in my hands, and I apologized to God for being so inferior, *so not enough.*

As soon as I uttered the words, I felt such a strong and ferocious response on the inside of my insides. I felt like God said, "*I don't make inferior things*!"

At that point, I had never felt His presence so strongly.

This was part of the beginning of my healing journey; healing from abuse, trauma, and breaking the dysfunctional patterns of generations before me.

God doesn't make inferior things, became something I repeated to myself often.

For even if other people around me treated me as less than, God did not think of me that way. And I had to come to a place where His voice became greater in me than the voices of my past.

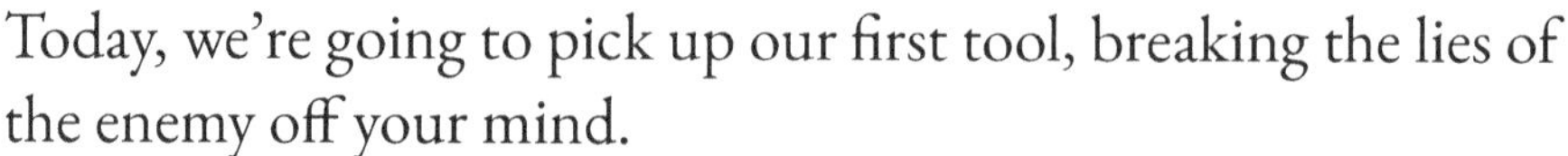

Today, we're going to pick up our first tool, breaking the lies of the enemy off your mind.

Reflect

Write Ephesians 1:4 here:

According to this verse, when did God choose you?

What is going on in your heart and mind as you realize this?

Have you experienced not feeling chosen? Explain.

Tool

The first tool in our toolbox is breaking the lies we have believed off our hearts and minds. Read the prayer below silently, and if it resonates with you, pray it from your heart out loud to God.

> In the name of Jesus, I break the power of the lie of rejection off my life. I declare the truth that My Heavenly Father chose me before the foundation of the world. I am not rejected; I am chosen by the King of all Kings and Lord of all Lords. Father God, any place where rejection has wrapped itself around my heart or took up residence in my mind, I pray that You would bring Your healing touch even now. In Jesus' mighty name, amen.

Walk It Out In Everyday Life

To use this tool in everyday life, first recognize those little fleeting thoughts, thoughts of not enough or negative things about yourself.

Write down a truth from God's Word that refutes that thought, and when those negative thoughts come, stop, and say:

In the name of Jesus, I break that lie. I declare the truth (and declare the truth of the Word of God out loud).

Forgiven

Read: Ephesians 1:6-10

I still remember that first day of college.

It started with chapel, and the faculty invited all the new students to come to the front for prayer.

I stepped forward, and this big teddy bear of a man stood over me, placing his hands on my head. He said a few words in prayer, and then the words that I will never forget came out of his mouth, "That's not who you are anymore! When God looks at you, He sees the righteousness of Jesus Christ!"

I had made mistakes in my past, poor decisions that affected my life. Some toxic people around me made sure to mention those mistakes at every opportunity, never letting me forget.

But God was speaking to my heart so strongly that day.

Those mistakes, those poor choices, were not who I was anymore. God was calling me to let go of the guilt, shame and condemnation and realize that in Him I could find forgiveness and a new way of living life with Him.

That day was the start of a new season for me, and it started with the words, "That's not who you are anymore."

Today, we'll talk about some things we have in Christ, one of them being the forgiveness of sins.

Reflect

Write Ephesians 1:7 here:

Underline what it says you have "in Him".

Look up 1 John 1:9 and write it here:

Have you made mistakes that you aren't proud of? Have you, like me, been reminded of those mistakes again and again by people that wanted to define you by those mistakes, never letting you grow into anything better?

Tool

The second tool in our toolbox is taking off false labels, this one being the label of *unforgivable.*

If you have felt defined by your mistakes, or struggled with feeling forgiven, pray this prayer with me and take off that label. Pray the prayer silently to yourself, and if it resonates with you, pray it from your heart out loud to God.

> In the name of Jesus, I surrender the label of unforgivable, shamed, condemned, and guilty. I break the power of those labels off me now, and I forgive those who labeled me as such. I take that label off, and I ask Father God, in Jesus' name, that you would define me by Your love. I pray that You would help me walk free of anyone's labels, or any guilt, shame or condemnation that goes with them. In the name of Jesus Christ I pray, amen.

Walk It Out In Everyday Life

When you feel labeled by others, lift your face to the Lord and thank Him that He died for your sins. Remind yourself that if you have confessed your sins to Him, He is faithful and just to forgive you and cleanse you of all unrighteousness (See 1 John 1:9). Thank Him that when He looks at you, He sees the righteousness of Jesus Christ (See 2 Corinthians 5:21).

It Will Work Out

Read Ephesians 1:11

"I ask Father, that you would wipe the burdens from Carolyn's shoulders. Those burdens are not hers to carry," the pastor prayed.

Carrying burdens had been normal to me, especially the burden of trying to make everyone else happy, fix things, and make sure that no one was upset with me.

I didn't quite understand what he prayed at the moment, but as I moved along on my healing journey, I learned about boundaries, and that other people's happiness was not my responsibility.

I learned that it's ok to say no, and to not carry every burden people placed on me.

When burdens try to come on me now, especially the burden of fear, worry or anxiety, I have to be intentional about laying them down and giving those burdens into God's hands.

The verse that we are going to learn about today is one that will be so helpful if you struggle with carrying the burden of worry or fear.

Reflect

Read Ephesians 1:11 again slowly. Particularly the part about God working things out according to His will.

Quiet your heart and mind for a moment and ask the Holy Spirit to speak to you about this verse. You can say something as simple as, "Holy Spirit, please speak to my heart about this verse and make it real to me."

What is going on in your heart during these quiet moments?

Are there situations in your life that have seemed so bleak you've wondered if they could ever be worked out at all?

Tool

The tool we are picking up today is lifting the burdens we carry into God's hands. We'll implement this tool with the following prayer. Read it silently to yourself, and if it resonates with you, pray it out loud from your heart to God.

> Father God, I give You this burden I've been carrying. I choose to wipe the burden of this situation off my shoulders, and I declare that it is Your burden to bear, and not mine. Father, I pray for Your wisdom in this situation, and that You'd direct my steps. Thank You that Your Word says when I ask for wisdom, You give it liberally without finding fault (See James 1:5). Thank You, Father, that You work this situation out according to Your purpose and will. I let go of trying to make anything happen or control it in any way. I leave it in Your hands, and I choose to trust You with it. In Jesus' mighty name, amen.

Walk It Out In Everyday Life

When you feel yourself holding burdens that aren't yours, or you're struggling with anxiety or fear, pray this prayer daily, even several times a day if needed.

Sealed

Read Ephesians 1:12-14

Have you ever felt all alone in a room full of people?

I have.

For me, it came from feeling misunderstood, rejected, or not wanting to open up because of fear or anxiety.

The root of it all was being abandoned as a child, physically and emotionally. I spent a lot of time alone, fending for myself.

I felt that abandonment well into adulthood, especially when I didn't know how to do basic things that people were taught in childhood.

But I learned that there was One who never left me during that entire time. I found comfort at the feet of Jesus, and He helped me to walk free of that feeling of loneliness.

It's easy to believe that God has abandoned you when you're going through hard things. Today, we are going to look further at the truth of God's Word and then break any lie we may have believed that said we were abandoned or alone in this world.

Reflect

I'm sharing our passage from today in the NIV, because there is some wording in this version that I want to focus on today.

12 In order that we, who were the first to put our hope in Christ, might be for the praise of his glory.

13 And you also were included in Christ when you heard the message of truth, the gospel of your salvation. When you believed, you were marked in him with a seal, the promised Holy Spirit,

14 who is a deposit guaranteeing our inheritance until the redemption of those who are God's possession—to the praise of his glory.

Ephesians 1:12-14 NIV

When you heard the message of truth, what does verse 13 say that you are?

And what are you marked with?

Who does verse 14 say the Holy Spirit is?

What does this verse speak to your heart about Who is with you?

Look up Psalm 139:1-18

As you read, notice the verses that speak about God always being with you.

Look up Deuteronomy 31:8.

Where does this say God is, and what He will never do?

What do these verses speak to your heart about not being alone?

No matter what you've been through, no matter how rejected you have felt, you have never walked the path alone. Even if you can't feel Him, even if it seems so dark, the Word says the darkness is as light to Him (See Psalm 139:12). He sees you; He knows you, and you are never ever alone.

Tool

The tool for today is breaking the lie that you've been abandoned or alone. We'll implement this tool by praying the following prayer. Read the prayer silently to yourself, and if it resonates with you, pray it out loud from your heart to God.

> In the name of Jesus, I break the power of the lie that I have been abandoned by God. I thank You Lord, that even if I didn't feel You, You have always been with me. You have not rejected me, but I was included in Christ when I believed in You. I declare the truth that the Holy Spirit is always with me. I pray that this truth will become more real to me than any lie I have believed. In Jesus' mighty name, amen.

Walk It Out In Everyday Life

When the lie comes to your mind that you've been alone, abandoned or rejected, say:

I reject that lie, and I declare the truth that the Holy Spirit is always present with me. I am never ever alone.

Paul's Prayer

Read Ephesians 1:15-21

Something I struggled with as a growing Christian was the thought that no matter how much I read, or how much I prayed, that it was not enough. I had heard that the Word of God could heal my hurting heart, and I wasn't healed yet, so I must need more of it!

I had this fear come to mind almost daily, that I wasn't doing it right.

I pushed myself to be the best pray-er, the best Bible reader, and the best at memorizing Scripture. I literally wore myself out to the point that I had no energy left.

One day, a pastor sat down with me and said, "I want you to stop reading your Bible for one week. Take a rest. Then, I want you to take it one bite, one piece at a time."

Not long after, I saw this picture in my mind of someone stuffing so much food in their face that they didn't even have enough time to chew. The food was just falling out of their mouth. But when they took one small bite at a time, they had time to chew their food, and nothing fell out of their mouth.

This is when I learned that healing comes by taking small daily steps with the Lord. I didn't need to work hard enough or do enough. I just needed to enjoy the presence of my Heavenly

Father and know that He accepted me just as I was, broken and all.

It was His gift of Jesus Christ that made me enough.

During this time of taking in the Scriptures slowly, thinking about them and turning them over in my mind, I learned the power of praying the Scriptures back to God.

Today, we're going to look at one of Paul's prayers, and pray that prayer back to God for ourselves.

Reflect

In verse 17, what does Paul ask the Ephesians to be given?

Why did He ask it?

In verse 18, what does Paul pray about the eyes of the heart?

And what does he pray that they would know? (Verses 18-19)

In your own words, what do verses 19- 20 say about that "incomparably great power for us who believe" (NIV)?

Tool

The Tool we are going to pick up today is praying the Scriptures back to God. Look at the things you've just written down that Paul asked for the Ephesians and what he wanted them to know.

Then write out your own prayer to God, using the points listed as a guide, and pray that prayer from your heart out loud to your Heavenly Father in the name of Jesus Christ.

Walk It Out In Everyday Life

When you come across a scripture that especially speaks to your heart, you can take the points of that Scripture and turn them into a prayer to pray back to God.

Under His Feet

Read Ephesians 1:22-23

It felt like our world was falling apart.

The situation in our family had become so dark as we watched someone we loved pulled away from church, family, even away from friendships they'd had for years. The person they were with seemed to be isolating them from everyone and filling their head with lies.

I wanted desperately to save our family member, but any attempts were met with hateful words and more distance.

So, I watched and prayed from afar, often with many tears, as they continued down this dark pit of destruction.

I quickly found that if I did not commit this situation over to God and declare that He was bigger than this situation, it consumed my thoughts, and fear ruled my days.

It became warfare for me, fighting between what I saw happening and trying to believe the promises God had given me, even though it looked just the opposite.

Several times a day I raised my hands to Heaven, and declared God's truth over this situation, asking for God's help to leave it in His hands. During that dark time, before we saw God move, it was the only way I had any peace.

Reflect

Write Ephesians 1:22 here:

Where are "all things" according to this Scripture?

Have you had circumstances in your life that wouldn't seem to go away, or just got worse, seeming like huge mountains to you?

What does this Scripture speak to your heart about those situations?

Take a few moments and think about this Scripture. If you're in a place where it's safe to do so, close your eyes and picture the words in your mind.

Then, picture the situations in your life under the feet of Jesus.

What is going on in your heart as you think upon this Scripture?

Tool

The Tool we'll be picking up today is declaring that God is bigger than the situations we face.

Read the following prayer silently to yourself, and if it resonates with you, pray it from your heart, out loud to God.

> In the name of Jesus, I declare that this situation is not bigger than You, but it is under Your feet. I pray for Your wisdom if there's anything for me to do here, and if there's not, I pray for Your peace as I am still and know that You fight for me (See Exodus 14:14). I thank You for reminding me of Your promises and helping me to have courage as I face situations that seem bigger than me. Give me the courage to leave this situation in Your hands. In Jesus' mighty name, amen.

Walk It Out In Everyday Life

If you find yourself in a situation that seems like a mountain, declare that the situation is under the feet of Jesus.

Made Alive in Christ

Read Ephesians 2:1-5

For many years, I lived as though I was still in the darkness.

With a family background in the occult, the darkness of the past pelted me with lies. I had given place to the things of the demonic, and they were not leaving willingly. It felt as if I took one step forward with God, but the darkness and demonic dragged me three steps backward, trying to hold on to me.

But because of God's grace, He directed my steps to a ministry who knew exactly how to help me out of the spiritual warfare I found myself in.

This ministry helped me understand, that because of Jesus' blood shed for me, I was no longer dead in those things, but Christ was alive and well in me and I could walk free of the things I'd been involved in.

On one particular day, I received prayer from a woman, and as she prayed, I felt a physical release from the darkness that had been hovering over me. When she finished praying, she firmly said, "Christ is *in you*! That same power is *in you*!"

I didn't comprehend at the time that I was alive in Christ. I had accepted salvation, but I still lived in the darkness of yesterday.

But because of God's great love for me, He led me step-by-step into the understanding and knowledge of His power alive in me.

Today's reading is about this very thing: being saved from our old ways and made alive in Christ by God's great love for you.

Reflect

What does this passage say you once were (verse 2:1)?

What does it say you are now (Verse 2:5)?

Salvation is a gift given to you by your Heavenly Father, who loves you with an everlasting love (See Jeremiah 31:3).

If you have struggled with believing God loves you, read the following verses out loud, then read the prayer silently to yourself, and if it resonates with you, pray it out loud from your heart to God.

The Lord has appeared of old to me, *saying:* Yes, I have loved you with an everlasting love; Therefore with lovingkindness I have drawn you (Jeremiah 31:3 NKJV).

What then shall we say to these things? If God *is* for us, who *can be* against us (Romans 8:31 NKJV)?

"Come now, and let us reason together, "Says the Lord, "Though your sins are like scarlet, they shall be as white as snow; Though they are red like crimson, They shall be as wool (Isaiah 1:18 NKJV).

Instead of your shame *you shall have* double *honor,* and *instead of* confusion they shall rejoice in their portion. Therefore, in their land they shall possess double; Everlasting joy shall be theirs (Isaiah 61:7 NKJV).

Prayer

Father God, I pray that You would help me to know that I am loved beyond measure, that You are for me and not against me. I surrender to You the experiences I've had in this life that affected my belief in You, and in my self-worth. Wash me of the things that have made me feel unclean before You and ashamed before others. Help me lift my face to You, unashamed, knowing that once I was in darkness, but now I am in Your light, and am made alive in Christ because of Your great love for me. In Jesus' mighty name, amen.

Tool

The tool we are going to pick up today is writing down the truth and keeping it before us.

Write down the truth that you are no longer dead in your sins, that you are alive in Christ because of God's great love for you. Take five minutes of any part of your day to look at that truth, speak it out loud to yourself, and think about that truth and what it means to you.

Walk It Out In Everyday Life

When things from the past come up that would try to tell you something other than the truth of God's Word, praise Your Heavenly Father that He saved you out of that past by His great love for you and that you are made alive in Christ by His grace.

We Are God's Workmanship

Read Ephesians 2:6-10

Perfection.

I tried to never make a mistake.

Because of the constant criticism I experienced growing up, I felt that no matter what I did or accomplished, I was never good enough.

Even if I didn't physically experience someone standing over me with condemning words and accusing eyes anymore, the voices still lived in my head.

When I made a mistake, I felt like I had failed miserably, and my worth and value became wrapped up in my performance and accomplishments.

Awards, certificates, a degree, and other accomplishments covered my office wall. Yet, the voices still lived in my head, screaming, *not good enough!*

My Heavenly Father's voice said something different. God whispered to me that I *was* good enough.

It seemed completely backwards from what I'd grown up with... but soon, the whispers of God's truth started to get louder than the screams in my head, and the whispers are still getting louder, even today.

When I catch myself in performance mode, or if a goal isn't quite being reached on time, I remind myself that I am not what I accomplish, that my worth and value is not based on what I do, or on what other people say. My worth and value is based on the fact that My Heavenly Father loves me with all His heart, and He is doing the work in me.

I don't have to try to be perfect anymore, I just need to bask in His love.

Reflect

Have you ever felt like you had to be perfect? To do all the work, to earn the love you so want?

Write Ephesians 2:8-9:

What does this say about having to earn God's love?

Write Ephesians 2:10.

According to this verse, what are we?

Which means *Who* does the work?

Dear sister in Christ, He already loves you.

You don't have to work hard enough or be enough to be loved. And if you make a mistake, you are not condemned. Come to your Heavenly Father, ask His forgiveness, and for His help to do better next time.

You are loved.

You are adored.

You don't have to work for God's love.

Tool

The tool we are going to pick up today is letting the Heavenly Father Speak to your heart.

Find a quiet moment and ask the Holy Spirit to speak to your heart about God's great love for you. Sit quietly with your eyes closed, if you can, for the next five minutes or so. Write down what comes to your heart and mind.

Walk It Out In Everyday Life

Whenever you feel that need for perfection, stop for a moment, and ask the Lord to speak to your heart about His great love for you.

Brought Near by His Blood

Read Ephesians 2:11-16

The enemy likes to lie to you.

He brings negative thoughts, people who aren't walking with God, even circumstances. And to hurt you most of all, he'll bring religious people with their legalism to try and bring shame and condemnation into your life.

He will try to make you live less than you are and leave you stuck thinking that you are abandoned and alone in this life.

The enemy of all that is good is afraid of you taking your place, of who you are, of your authority, and of you walking in the truth. Why? Because when you do, it puts one more dent of destruction in his kingdom.

He's afraid of who you really are, and he knows that when you take your rightful place and stand as a daughter of the King of all Kings and Lord of all Lords, he's done for.

Who are you? And by what power do you walk?

Let's take a look today.

Reflect

Write Ephesians 2:13 here:

What does this verse say you used to be?

And what does it say you are now?

By what power?

Look up the following verses and write down anything that especially speaks to your heart when you read them.

2 Corinthians 5:17

Romans 5:9-10

1 Corinthians 6:11

Colossians 1:13-14

Tool

The tool we are going to pick up today is praying the blood of Jesus. Read the following prayer to yourself silently, and if it resonates with you, pray it from your heart, out loud to God.

> I thank you Jesus that you shed your blood on the cross for me so that I could be brought near to You. Thank you that through your death and resurrection I am no longer dead in my sins, but I am made alive in You. Help me to know that this is a gift from you, and I don't have to earn it, only receive it. Thank You, that through the gift of your blood shed for me, I have been made new, that I am justified by your blood, forgiven of my sins, saved from wrath, and reconciled to God the Father. Thank You, that I am washed by the blood of the lamb, delivered from the power of darkness, and brought into the Kingdom of God. I receive this gift of Your blood shed for me, Jesus. Help me to walk in confidence as

a daughter of the King of all Kings through the gift of your blood shed for me. Amen.

Walk It Out In Everyday Life

When any lies come your way, trying to tell you that you're not forgiven, not worthy, or anything else contrary to the Word, say out Loud:

"I am made new, forgiven, and whole by the blood of Jesus through His death and resurrection. Darkness has no hold on me anymore because I am set free from darkness by the power of Jesus' blood."

No Longer Outside Looking In

Read Ephesians 2:17-22

For years, feelings of unworthiness, not being good enough, rejection and abandonment clung to me. On one particular day, I sat with my Bible in the living room, and wrote in my journal about what I'd just read.

Now, I can't remember the verse I read that day, but I remember writing in my journal how I felt like I didn't measure up to that truth. I look back with such sadness of what I thought of myself.

Sometimes our experiences, or how we've been treated by others, can cause us to argue with the very truth of who God says we are in His Word. We have a hard time believing it because we've been lied to for so long.

Today, we are going to pick up a tool that will help us talk back to the lies that have robbed us of walking in the confidence of Whose we are.

Reflect

In verse 18, Who does it say we have access to?

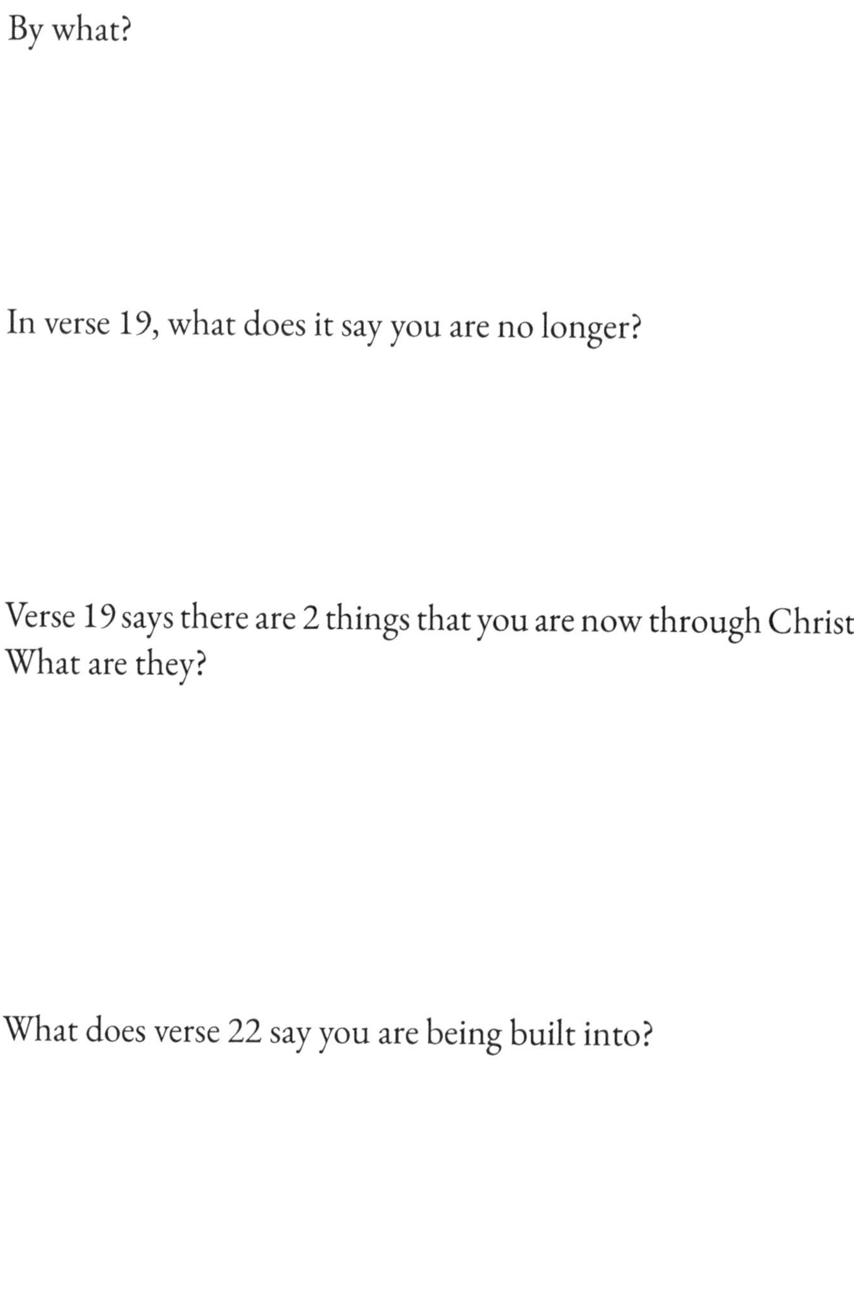

By what?

In verse 19, what does it say you are no longer?

Verse 19 says there are 2 things that you are now through Christ. What are they?

What does verse 22 say you are being built into?

What is going on in your heart as you realize these things?

Tool

The tool we are picking up today is declaring God's truth over ourselves and our lives. If you have been struggling with feeling unwanted, insignificant, or not worthy of God's love, write down the truth of the verses we have just gone over and put them some place you will see them every day. Declare them out loud to yourself for the next 30 days.

I also invite you to read this prayer silently to yourself and if it resonates with you, pray it from your heart, out loud to God.

> In the name of Jesus, I lift my heart, mind, and emotions before you Father God, and I ask for Your healing touch on my life, especially the parts where I have not been included, have been made to feel less than or insignificant in any way. Help me to walk in the confidence that I am included and worthy because of Christ's gift to me, and that I am being built up together with other citizens of Christ to be a dwelling place for your Spirit. Thank you, Father,

that You want to heal me, that you do not see me as insignificant, and that you love me more than I could ever imagine. In Jesus' mighty name I pray, amen.

Walk It Out In Everyday Life

When feelings of insignificance or unworthiness come, talk back to those thoughts and feelings by declaring the truth of what God's Word says.

The Mystery

Read Ephesians 3:1-6

I felt like I didn't belong.

People came and said hello that day at church, hugged me, asked how our family was, and were genuinely interested in me. I smiled and chatted, but inside, my heart was heavy and hurting.

The trauma and rejection I'd experienced still laid their claim on my heart.

At the end of church, I sat at the altar in prayer, asking the Lord to *please* heal me, to take the pain away.

I believed a lie that had gone down to my very core. No matter how loved or accepted I was, I still felt that rejection, that feeling of not belonging.

Today, we are going to take the first step in breaking the lie that you do not belong.

Reflect

Read Ephesians 3:6 again.

Write down the three things this verse says the Gentiles are.

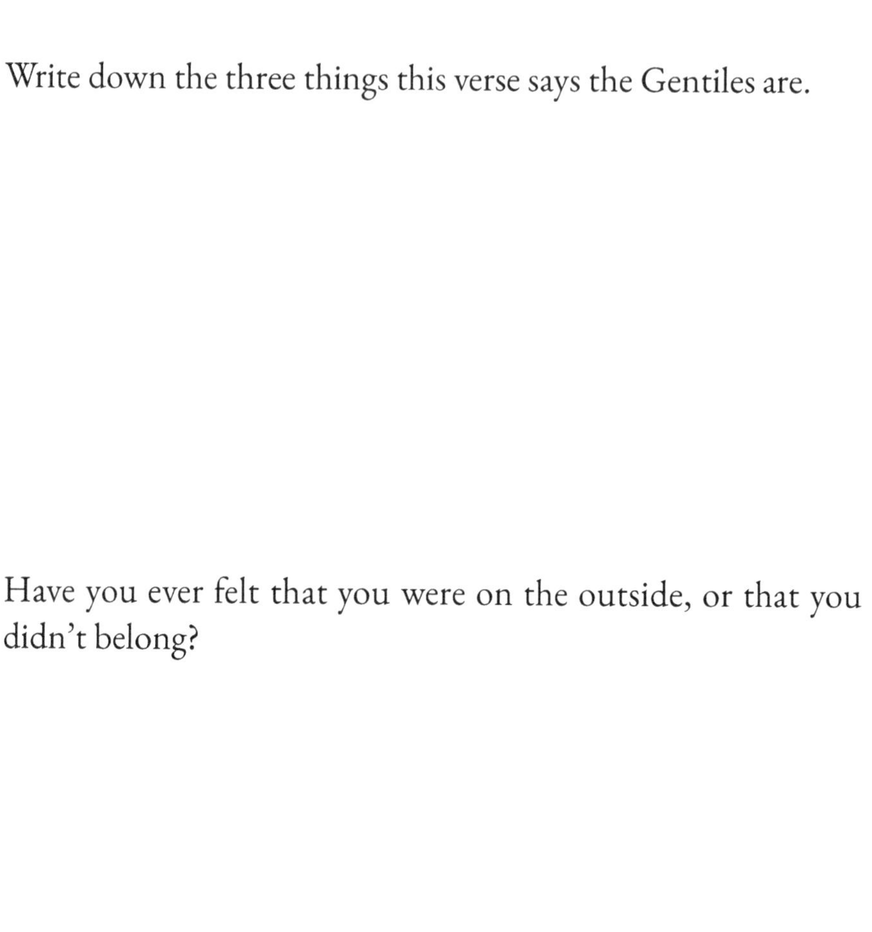

Have you ever felt that you were on the outside, or that you didn't belong?

Tool

The tool we are going to pick up today is asking God to not let those lies live in our minds anymore and to fill you with the knowledge of His love for you.

Read the following prayer to yourself silently, and if it resonates with you, pray it out loud from your heart to God.

> Father God, I surrender to You the feeling of being rejected and not belonging. I break the power of

these lies off my mind and break that lying spirit of rejection off my heart. In the name of Jesus, I command the lies to be uprooted from my life.

Father God, I pray that You would help me to grow in confidence of who I am in You. Give me encouragement and help me to heal from the past. Help me to grow in the knowledge of the depth of Your love for me. Help me to look at myself not through the lenses of how others have treated me, letting them define who I am, but help me to look through the lenses of Your great love for me, and who You've created me to be. In Jesus' mighty name, amen.

Walk It Out In Everyday Life

When you feel that rejection try to take hold, declare the truths from these Scriptures.

I am an heir of Christ; I am a member of Christ's body and I belong. The promises God has made to Israel also belong to me. I am a daughter of the King of all Kings and Lord of all Lords, and I belong. There is a place at His table for me.

Freedom and Confidence

Read Ephesians 3:7-12

That day, as I approached the altar, one of the pastors asked me a few questions about my prayer need. Then, as he prayed, he started naming things in my life that I hadn't told him about, nor would he have any way of knowing. But it was the last words he prayed that stuck with me for years to come. "God is not angry! God is not angry!"

I had grown up in a household with alcoholism, anger, and abuse. I lived with the constant fear of doing or saying the wrong thing, so I was literally afraid to move.

My voice became just a whisper, so that later in life, people could barely hear me at all.

I was so fearful of being seen or heard, lest I meet with that anger.

So, that pastor praying and declaring that God was not angry at me spoke volumes.

Over the course of time, as I followed Jesus, my Heavenly Father showed me that He truly wasn't angry, but in fact, was just the opposite.

Today we are picking up the tool of asking God to show us who He truly is, and to heal us from the wounds left upon our hearts by people who didn't represent Him well.

Reflect

Write Ephesians 3:12 here.

Underline what God has given us through faith in Jesus.

What is going on in your heart as you realize this truth?

What was your earthly father or father figure like? Was he an example of who God is, or an example of what God isn't?

Tool

The tool we are picking up today is asking God to heal our wounded hearts.

If your earthly father or father figure wounded you in any way, I invite you to pray this prayer, forgiving him, and asking God to heal your wounded heart. Read the prayer silently to yourself, and if it resonates with you, pray it out loud from your heart to God.

> In the name of Jesus, I choose to forgive those in my life who held the title of father or father figure for treating me as less than the precious daughter God made me to be. I choose to forgive him for not representing God well, and for all the pain and heartache he caused in my life. I pray, Father God, that if it made me fear being seen or heard, or I have hidden my true self, I pray that You would heal me. Help me come out of hiding, and know that You see me, You hear me, and that You are not angry, but are pleased with me. Heal my heart of all the words and actions that pierced my soul, robbing me of my self-worth and freedom to be who I am. In Jesus' mighty name, I pray, amen.

Walk It Out In Everyday Life

On a daily basis, raise your face to look at the sky like you are looking up to Heaven and say out loud to your Heavenly Father,

"You are my Father. I am your daughter. Thank you for showing me who You really are, and how precious I am to you."

Rooted and Grounded

Read Ephesians 3:13-19

I had never felt the love of God so powerfully before.

I was sitting in prayer, and I had the strongest feeling that this woman I knew needed to be reminded that God loved her. I didn't have her number, but I had her email, so I started typing an encouraging message to her.

As I typed this message out, I felt this great love come into the room with me. There are no words to describe what I felt, except maybe tangible, mighty, overpowering... such love as I'd never felt before.

That moment gave *me* a picture of God's love. Our Father in Heaven loves each one of us so ferociously, a tangible love that never ends.

Today we come upon a prayer that Paul prays for the Ephesians, and we will take a look at what he prays about knowing God's love.

Reflect

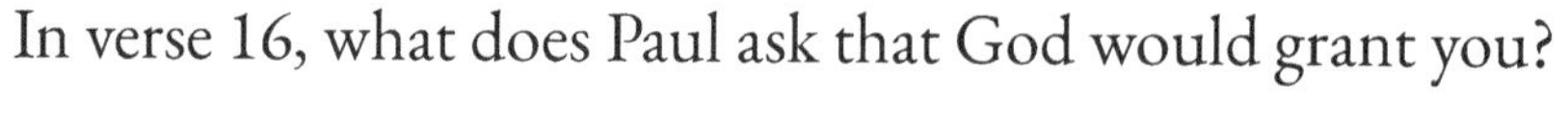

In verse 16, what does Paul ask that God would grant you?

In verse 17, where does He ask that Christ dwell?

And for you to be rooted and grounded in what?

Let's look at that word rooted for a moment.

In Strong's Lexicon, rooted is defined as:

"To cause to strike root, to strengthen with roots, to render firm, to fix, establish, cause a person or a thing to be thoroughly grounded" [1]

And the word Grounded in Strong's lexicon is defined as:

"to lay the foundation, to found to make stable, establish"[2]

Let's apply that to ourselves for a moment.

Paul is praying for us to be rooted and grounded.

Write down in your own words, from the Strong's definition of the words rooted and grounded, what that means to you to be rooted and grounded in God's love.

---

1. "G4492 - rhizoō - Strong's Greek Lexicon (kjv)." Blue Letter Bible. Web. 2 Mar, 2023. <https://www.blueletterbible.org/lexicon/g4492/kjv/tr/0-1/>.

2. "G2311 - themelioō - Strong's Greek Lexicon (kjv)." Blue Letter Bible. Web. 2 Mar, 2023. <https://www.blueletterbible.org/lexicon/g2311/kjv/tr/0-1/>.

And in verse 18 -19, what does Paul pray that you would know?

In Verse 19, Paul says why he is praying this, so that you may be filled with what?

Pause and think about this for a moment, Dear Sister! Paul is saying, when we know and comprehend God's love, it fills us with His power!

When people find themselves in a battle of some sort or they experience tragedy or loss, what is the first thing many people question?

God's love.

The enemy would like you to think you are not loved and that you've lost the love of God somehow.

And why?

Because when you comprehend and know the love of God, when you are filled with God's love, and are sure of it, you are full of God's power!

The enemy has tried to make you feel unloved, because he wants to make sure you are not walking in God's power.

What is going on in your heart as you read these words, Dear Sister, as you realize what the enemy was *really* after in your life?

Tool

The tool we are picking up today is praying Paul's prayer for ourselves. I've written an example out below, but feel free to use the points listed above and write out your own prayer to God.

> Example Prayer:
>
> Father God, in the name of Jesus, I ask that You strengthen me by Your Holy Spirit in my inner being. I invite Christ to dwell fully in my heart, and that I would be rooted and grounded in the love of Christ, comprehending, and knowing that love which goes beyond anything I've ever imagined, that I may be filled with the fullness of God.

Walk It Out In Everyday Life

Anytime you feel unloved or question if you matter, ask the Father to remind you of His love. You could say something like, "Father, please remind me of Your great love for me today. In Jesus' name, amen."

More Than We Can Ask or Imagine

Read Ephesians 3:20-21

I used to think that if I could please everybody, *that* was walking in love.

As a child who grew up in a dysfunctional environment, I was taught that I was responsible for others' happiness, and that if I did anything for myself, it was selfish and unloving.

On my journey of healing, I learned that it's ok to have boundaries, and that to fill my own cup first *is* loving. I cannot give effectively when I am empty.

Dear Sister, walking in love is *not* people pleasing.

Galatians 1:10 says, "If I were still trying to please people, I would not be a servant of Christ" (NIV).

I pray that as you read the verses today and pray to be filled with more of God's love, that you would find freedom from feeling like you must please everyone and never take care of yourself.

Reflect

According to verse 20, what is God able to do?

And what is it according to?

Remember what we learned yesterday about God's power and being rooted and grounded in love.

Look up 2 Timothy 1:7.

According to this verse, what are 3 things that God gives us?

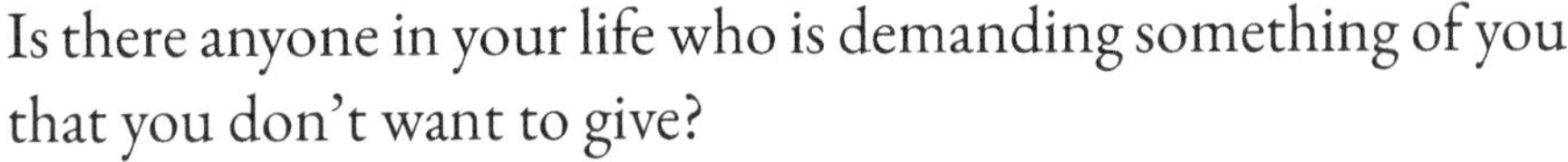

Is there anyone in your life who is demanding something of you that you don't want to give?

Look up 2 Corinthians 9:7.

What does this verse say you should give?

And what does it say you should not give out of?

God's love and His power work together. But one thing I had to learn, and I so want you to know, is that being loving does not mean you have to give until you have nothing left or put up with manipulation, control, or abuse.

Tool

Today we are going to pick up the tool of believing that God can do more than we can ask or imagine, according to His power that works within us. And the first step to picking up that tool is praying for more of God's love in our lives.

Read the following prayer silently, and if resonates with you, pray it out loud from your heart to God; Or feel free to write your own prayer to God.

> Father God, in the name of Jesus, I repent for anytime I did not walk in love toward others, and I choose to forgive those who did not walk in love toward me. I surrender them into Your hands. I ask that You help me not to be stopped up or held captive by offense, but to trust that You are my defender and vengeance is Yours. I repent for any place I have wanted others to suffer for what they've done, instead of walking in forgiveness and letting You handle it. Lord, teach me what it means to walk in love, that it's ok to say no to those who try to coerce me into doing what *they* want. Help me to walk in love toward myself as well and give only what I have decided in my heart to give. Please remove from me anywhere offense has taken root in my life and heal the places where I gave in to manipulation or control. In Jesus' mighty name, amen.

Walk It Out In Everyday Life

Any time you sense that you could grow in the area of love, remember that the trap of the enemy is offense, and ask the Lord to help you walk in love, have boundaries, and give only what you have decided in your heart to give.

Note

Remember that walking in love does not mean you put yourself in harmful situations or don't have boundaries. If you are struggling with any situation where you want to walk in love, but you are being hurt, please get help from a trusted professional who can help you walk through setting boundaries and taking care of yourself.

Worthy of the Calling

Reading for the Day: Ephesians 4:1-6

In Verse 4:1 in the NIV, it says "live a life worthy of the calling you have received".

To live a life worthy of the calling, you must first know that you are called.

It's interesting that this word *calling* is used.

When I was growing up, the people around me called me things that were ugly and hurtful. Because of this, I felt unworthy, unloved, alone, and that I would never amount to anything worthy of praise.

But God.

As a young woman, I started poring over Scripture and listening to sermons that called me something different; chosen, treasured, forgiven, beautiful, loved, cherished, and many more.

How could I be these wonderful things when I had been called the opposite for so long?

Often, as human beings, and especially as children, we rise to the expectation of what we've been called.

What have you been called in your life?

But what has Jesus called you instead?

We often find out what Jesus calls us as we journey through the Word and get around people who have the fruit of the Spirit (see Galatians 5:22-23) in their lives.

Today, we are learning about living a life worthy of the calling you have received. Know that as you walk with the Lord, that calling becomes clearer, and the ungodly things you've been called in the past have less of an influence on your mind and heart.

Reflect

Ephesians 4:1 tells us what Paul urges us to do. What is it?

Verses 2 and 3 tell you *how* to live a life worthy of your calling. What are these verses telling you to do?

Which one of these things speaks to your heart the most?

Tool

The tool we're going to pick up today is listening for the Holy Spirit to speak to your heart. We'll start with a small prayer to pray.

Father God, I pray that You would speak to my heart through the Holy Spirit as I meditate on your Word today. In Jesus' name I pray, Amen.

Sit quietly for a moment and think about the passage you've just read. Wait on God for a moment and think about this verse.

What comes to your heart and mind as you sit quietly? Write it down if you wish.

Write out or say a prayer based on the Scripture you've meditated on and what you felt God spoke to your heart about it.

Is there a way you can apply the truth of this Scripture to Your Life? As an example, many times I will memorize Scriptures that say what God says about me.

Walk It Out In Everyday Life

You can implement these steps into your daily routine and make listening to the Holy Spirit a regular part of your life.

Just as a reminder, the steps are:

1. Find your verse.
2. Ask the Holy Spirit to speak to you about this verse.
3. Sit quietly while looking at this verse, writing down what comes to your mind and heart.
4. Pray the Scripture and what God spoke to you back to Him.
5. Is there a way to apply this Scripture to everyday life?

Gifts

Read Ephesians 4:7-13

When you have been treated badly, it's very easy to imagine that there's nothing good out there. And so, you isolate, keeping the bad out, but also keeping the good at bay.

I spent many a year, afraid to get into any relationship or let anyone see me. I felt the most alone in a room full of people because I was the quiet one who didn't talk and didn't interact.

But it was through spending time with Jesus that He gave me the courage to step out a little bit. I certainly didn't jump in with both feet, but I slowly tipped my toe into the water of entering healthy relationships.

God was building my confidence and working in my heart, so that I could discern between what was healthy and unhealthy. As I allowed Him to work in me, and with great fear, stepped out into what I had only known as hurtful, God led me to healthy people who became gifts to me.

Gifts of showing me what healthy was. Gifts of voices building me up instead of tearing me down. Gifts of people who prayed for me and truly wanted me to be the best that I could be.

As you read today, think about someone who is a gift in your life. And if you don't have anyone right now, ask God to send a healthy person into your life to be that gift to you.

Reflect

In verses 11-13, Paul states why Christ gave us certain people. Write down the reason why.

What is one way you have matured in your spiritual life recently?

Was there someone in your life who had an influence on that maturity?

On the other hand, is there someone in your life who has *not* built you up, but has torn you down and slowed your growth?

Who do you want to be around more, the one who helped you mature, or the one who tore you down?

How can you intentionally make more time for people who build you up?

Tool

The tool we are going to pick up today is forgiving those who have hurt us, even those in the church. Read the following prayer silently to yourself, and if it resonates with you, pray it out loud, from your heart to God.

> Father God, I choose to forgive those who should have been healthy examples, but instead, tore me down and caused me hurt or harm. I release each one of these into Your hands now. They are Your burden, and not mine. I refuse to carry the burden of their behavior anymore. Lord, I ask that You heal any brokenness in my life that was caused by people who were supposed to be gifts to me but chose to be something else instead. I ask Lord, that You would place people in my life that truly are gifts from You, and when You place them there, that You would give me the courage to trust again, and to heal. In Jesus' name I pray, amen.

Walk It Out In Everyday Life

Take note of the people in your life who are gifts to you and be intentional about the time you spend around them.

No Longer Infants

Read Ephesians 4:14-16

I did not come from a Christian home or background.

In fact, the environment I grew up in was filled with alcoholism, physical and emotional abuse, and books and things of the occult all around me.

I used to feel like I could just sense the darkness. But God, in His great mercy, called me out of that darkness and helped me to heal, to grow and to become mature in my faith; through Bible College, through ministries that guided me into healing, and through experiences and community that helped me to grow.

It wasn't always like that, though.

When I first came to Christ, I did not act like a mature Christian, nor did I know any kind of church etiquette. Certain people that held positions of authority rejected me and chose *not* to pour into me.

As painful as that was, I never stopped sitting at Christ's feet through His Word and through prayer. It was during these times that I felt the most loved and accepted.

It is Christ Himself, who has made a place for us at His table.

And that is what we are going to talk about today, becoming mature in Christ, and taking our place at the table He has set for us.

Reflect

In verse 14, what does Scripture say that infants in Christ are prone to?

And in verse 15, what should we be doing with the truth?

Verse 16 talks about every part of the body doing its work. Did you know that you have a part to play in the body of Christ? Whether you know what it is or not, you *do* have an important part to play.

What does verse 16 say what happens in the body of Christ as each part does its work?

Tool

The tool we are picking up today is choosing a habit, or spiritual discipline, that you would like to grow in, and asking God to help you implement that into your life in a way that fits the season you are in right now.

I included prayer, Scripture memorization, reading the Word, and journaling in my spiritual disciplines, one at a time, until they became habits. It certainly didn't happen overnight, and never happened perfectly. But I kept moving forward even if I didn't meet every goal.

You can choose anything that will help you grow closer to Christ.

What is one habit, or spiritual discipline, that you would like to grow in?

Taking into account what season you are in, how many days a week can you implement this practice? Make sure you do what blesses you, and not what is too much for you to carry right now.

Write out a prayer asking the Lord to help you grow in this area.

Walk It Out In Everyday Life

Something you could do, if you wish, is to track your progress on a calendar so that you can see how far you have come in growing in your good habits.

Put on the New

Read Ephesians 4:17-24

I was sure I couldn't do it.

But I felt like God was leading me to memorize Scripture. It kept coming to my mind, and would not go away.

So, I started to research *how* to memorize Scripture. I found that there are many methods, but one in particular stuck out to me, and that is the one I will share with you today. We'll pick up the tool of putting God's Word into our hearts and retaining what He has said to us.

If memorizing Scripture intimidates you, I'll show you an easy system to use that worked for me.

Reflect

According to verse 17, what is it that the Gentiles live in?

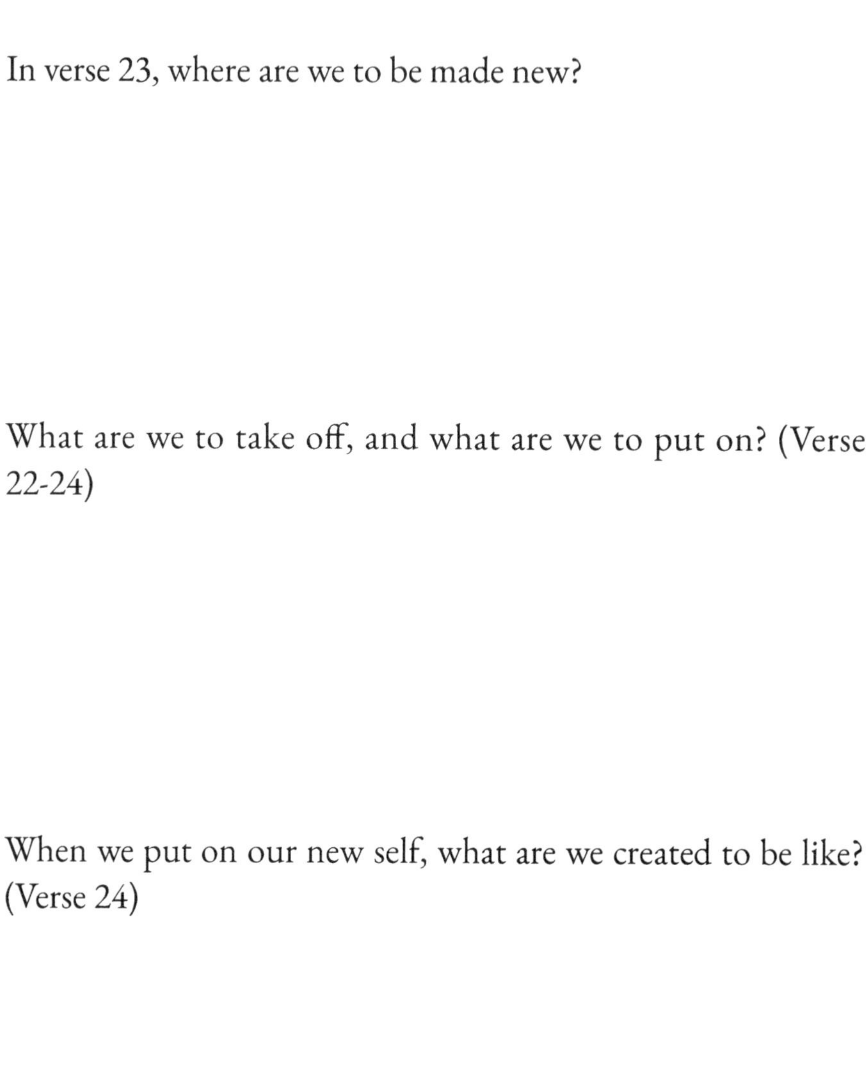

In verse 23, where are we to be made new?

What are we to take off, and what are we to put on? (Verse 22-24)

When we put on our new self, what are we created to be like? (Verse 24)

Tool

The tool we are going to pick up today is memorizing Scripture.

Say we are going to memorize John 3:16 in the NIV.

For God so loved the world that he gave his one and only Son, that whoever believes in him shall not perish but have eternal life.

1. We'll start by memorizing up to the first comma.

For God so loved the world that he gave his one and only Son,

Repeat that out loud ten times. I usually count on my fingers. After the first couple of times try not to look at the words.

1. Now, we will add the rest of the sentence after the comma.

For God so loved the world that he gave his one and only Son, that whoever believes in him shall not perish but have eternal life.

Repeat this verse ten times out loud, and after a few times, try not to look.

You can memorize any Scripture this way, going to the first comma, until you've finished the verse.

Walk It Out In Everyday Life

Choose a day that you would like to memorize one Scripture that has spoken to your heart, then review that Scripture at least once a day for the rest of the week.

Not Giving the Devil a Foothold

Read Ephesians 4:25-28

Once again, I rehearsed what they had done to me.

I was so angry, even bitter. The person who was supposed to love me the most in this world had allowed a monster into my life who caused me great pain, and then denied it ever happened.

My husband, who had listened to my venting many times before, said, "I really think you need to forgive them."

He was speaking the truth, but that truth made me even more angry when he said it. For years, I felt that if I hung on to the anger, it would somehow make them pay. But I was the one who was paying. I was the one stuck in hurt and anger, and the devil was gaining a foothold, tormenting me with thoughts about what had happened.

It was only when I gave it to God, choosing to trust that He would bring restoration and the justice I so wanted, that I started to heal.

I know firsthand it is difficult to let a wrong, especially a severe wrong, go. And there are feelings that need to be dealt with, let out, and not stuffed down. Yet, it is when we choose to let God into that space in our hearts and lives, that's when we truly begin to heal.

Today, we're going to reflect on what letting go of anger really means.

Reflect

In Ephesians 4:25, why do you think it's important to speak truthfully to your neighbor?

How could you implement this next time you have some hurt feelings or are angry?

Ephesians 4:26 says, "Do not let the sun go down while you are still angry," (NIV).

Have you met anyone who has let anger fester in their lives for a long time?

If so, what was the outcome for them?

Ephesians 4:27 explains why we're not to go to bed angry. Why do you think anger would give the devil a foothold in your life?

Tool

The tool we are going to pick up today is dealing with the anger in our lives. We will pray to the Lord to heal our hearts and lives of any anger we've allowed to fester.

Read the following prayer silently to yourself, and if it resonates with you, read it out loud from your heart to God.

> In the name of Jesus, I repent for allowing anger to fester in my life, and for walking in unforgiveness toward those who have wronged me. I break the power of anger over my life. I renounce any place I have given to anger, letting it fester, and any place I

have given the devil a foothold. In the name of Jesus, anger I close the door on you. You are not welcome here anymore in Jesus' mighty name. Father God, I pray that You would bring healing to my heart in those places where I was wronged. I thank You that You are a God of restoration, and I choose to trust You to make those wrongs right in Your time. Father, instead of hanging onto anger, I choose to forgive and to trust You to bring healing to my life. Help me to know what boundaries to have if the situation I'm angry about is still going on, and bring people into my life that would help me to heal. In Jesus' mighty name, amen.

Walk It Out In Everyday Life

When tormenting thoughts come, or you feel anger rising within you, surrender that anger or those thoughts to God once again. You could say something like, "Lord, I have forgiven those who wronged me. I give the anger up to You and trust You to bring justice and restoration to my life. In Jesus' name, amen"

Words

Read Ephesians 4:29-30

Even though I was only six years old, I remember that day vividly.

I waited in line for the bus to go home. When it arrived, I stepped up the big steps onto the bus, while the bus driver sat in the driver's seat watching each of us go by.

As I got to the place where I'd finally made it up the steps and was about to turn the corner to the aisle, the bus driver whispered to me, "You're the ugliest."

Being only six years old, I thought what this woman said was true. It must be, she was the adult in authority, and we were taught that what she said was final.

I found my seat next to the window, and looked out of it the entire way home, not talking to anyone. Not only was I dealing with what children should never see or have to deal with at home, now I had the bus driver telling me I was ugly.

Sometimes when we've had ugly words spoken over us, especially by authority figures, it can stay with us for a lifetime. Today, we're going to pick up the tool of breaking the power of ungodly words spoken over us and asking God to bring us to a place of healing.

Reflect

Are there words that were spoken over you that cut to your heart? Do they often play over and over in your mind?

If you can bring yourself to do so, write the word or sentence down here. We're going to pray over this in a moment and replace it with a better word.

Tool

Read the following prayer silently to yourself, and if it resonates with you, read it out loud from your heart to God. When you come to crossing out the ugly words, draw a line through what you've just written. This is a physical act representing what we are praying about.

> In the name of Jesus, I break the power of ungodly words spoken over me by others. I cross those words out and I renounce all agreements I have made with them. I ask you Father God, to uproot those ugly words from my heart and mind, and I pray that as I spend time in Your Word, that I would see and be able to receive what You say about me; that I am Your treasure, I am loved, and I am your pre-

cious daughter. I pray that Your truth would become more real to me than what anyone else has said. In Jesus' mighty name, amen.

Walk It Out In Everyday Life

When ungodly words come to your mind, speak the truth of what God says about you out loud. And if you want to go even further, speak what God says about you out loud daily while you're getting ready in the morning.

Bitterness and Anger

Read Ephesians 4:31-32

It's interesting that just a few verses ago, we read about anger, and now we are reading it here again, along with the word bitterness.

When someone crosses a boundary or wrongs you, it is natural to feel angry. And you may have a perfectly good and justifiable reason to be angry. But when we hang onto that anger, and don't make changes, such as setting some boundaries or talking about what happened to a trusted person, anger can quickly turn into bitterness.

I have held onto anger so long it became a pool of bitterness within me, and all I wanted to think or talk about were the wrongs that were done. I became trapped in this place of bitterness and could not let it go, until Jesus led me to people and ministries that helped me face it, and helped me to heal.

I know anger and bitterness can be a hard topic for some because you've been through such hard things, and have a perfect right to feel the way you do. But bear with me, and see if by the end of today's study, you are taking the first step of freedom from anger that wants to turn to bitterness.

Reflect

Have you been struggling with anger about something? Possibly it was something so unjust, and you have yet to see God move in that situation. You may even feel like the person or people got away with what they did.

What does the passage we have read today say to do about anger, bitterness, and rage?

Read Ephesians 4:26-27 one more time. What does it say can happen if you remain angry?

Look up John 10:10. What's the devil's purpose?

Look up Galatians 6:7. What does this verse say about what will happen to the person who wronged you, even if it hasn't happened yet?

Look up Hebrews 12:15. What does this say about a bitter root and what it does?

Tool

The tool we are going to pick up today is asking God to remove the anger, bitterness, and rage from our lives, and to show us healthy ways that we can respond when our boundaries have been crossed. Read the following prayer silently to yourself, and if it resonates with you, pray it out loud from your heart to God.

> Father God, I want to get rid of all anger, bitterness, and rage. I pray, Father, that You would lead me to counselors, ministries or other trusted people that can help me to heal and not let bitterness take root. Help me to know and discern who a safe person is for me, and to have wisdom in who to share with and who not to share with. I pray that You would cover every conversation I have, and that You would lead me to a place of freedom from bitterness. In Jesus' name I pray, amen.

Walk It Out In Everyday Life

If you struggle with anger that may have turned to bitterness, continue to surrender that anger as we've learned in Day 19, but also ask the Lord for wisdom and direction to help you heal.

What Not To Do

Read Ephesians 5:1-7

After putting boundaries up with some toxic people, I went up for prayer one morning after church. The pastor had spoken about ungodly words and invited people to come up who wanted healing from hurtful words.

As one of the prayer ministers prayed for me, he stopped and said, "I see a picture of a land that's barren and dark. You have planted seeds, but the ground has been toxic. But now that you have set boundaries, you will reap a harvest in your life. It's all been the same seed that you've been planting, but it was toxic ground. You are going to see your harvest come up."

I was so thankful for his words because I felt God had been speaking the same thing to my heart, and it was a confirmation for me.

I had been sowing obedience to the Word in my life, but I'd also been trying with all my might to make these toxic people happy. Instead of thinking about Jesus, and what *He* said about me, and what *He* wanted, I ruminated on these toxic people, trying to figure out why they acted the way they did, and what I could do to change things, as if *I* could somehow fix it.

Once I set boundaries and focused on getting healthy for myself, things began to change for me.

Today, we're going to talk about things and people God tells us to stay away from.

Reflect

After reading this passage, list out the things Paul tells us to ***not*** do.

Are any of these things a part of your life?

If so, you can pray the following prayer of surrender and repentance, asking God to help you walk in obedience to His Word. Read the prayer silently to yourself, and if it resonates with you, pray it out loud from your heart to God.

> Father God, I repent for the things listed here, (name each one) that have been a part of my life. I surrender these areas of my heart and life to You and ask You to help me be free of them. In Jesus' mighty name, amen.

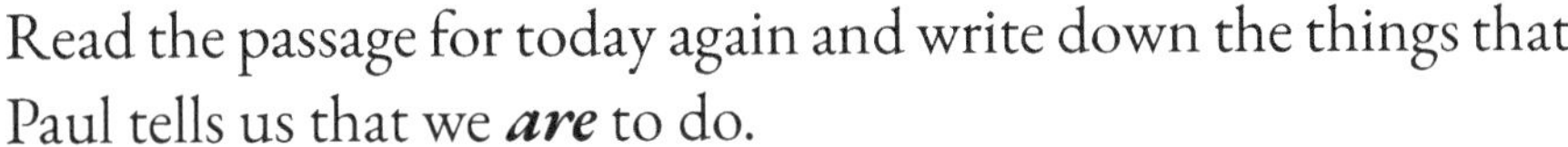

Read the passage for today again and write down the things that Paul tells us that we ***are*** to do.

How can you implement at least one of these into your life this week?

Tool

The tool we are going to pick up today is being mindful of applying the Word to every area of our lives, even in the area of relationships.

Look up the following verses about the company we are to keep and note the things that stand out to you.

1 Corinthians 15:33

Proverbs 1:10

Psalm 1:1-2

Take some time to pray about the relationships in your life. Ask your Heavenly Father if there is any place you are trying to fix things that only another person changing their attitudes or behavior can fix.

If you feel you need to make changes, seek wisdom and help from a trusted pastor, friend, or counselor.

Walk It Out In Everyday Life

When you read the Word of God, ask the Holy Spirit to speak to your heart about how to apply the Word to your daily life, even in the area of relationships.

Live as Children of Light

Read Ephesians 5:8-14

Picture in your mind a tree flourishing, living by a river of water, drawing life from that river. Then, picture a tree in the desert land, starving for water, producing no fruit, even dying.

In this passage, Paul is showing us how to live as children of light, and in the NIV, the word fruit is used twice in this passage.

Verse 9 says, "for the fruit of the light consists in all goodness, righteousness and truth."

And the other mention of fruit is in verse 11, "Have nothing to do with the fruitless deeds of darkness,"

We can accept Christ as our Savior and stop there, never growing, staying in the darkness, and having fruitless lives.

Or, we can live for Jesus, inviting Him into our everyday lives, growing in the knowledge of His Word and making choices according to His Word and His leading in our lives.

Reflect

In verse 8, what does it say you once were?

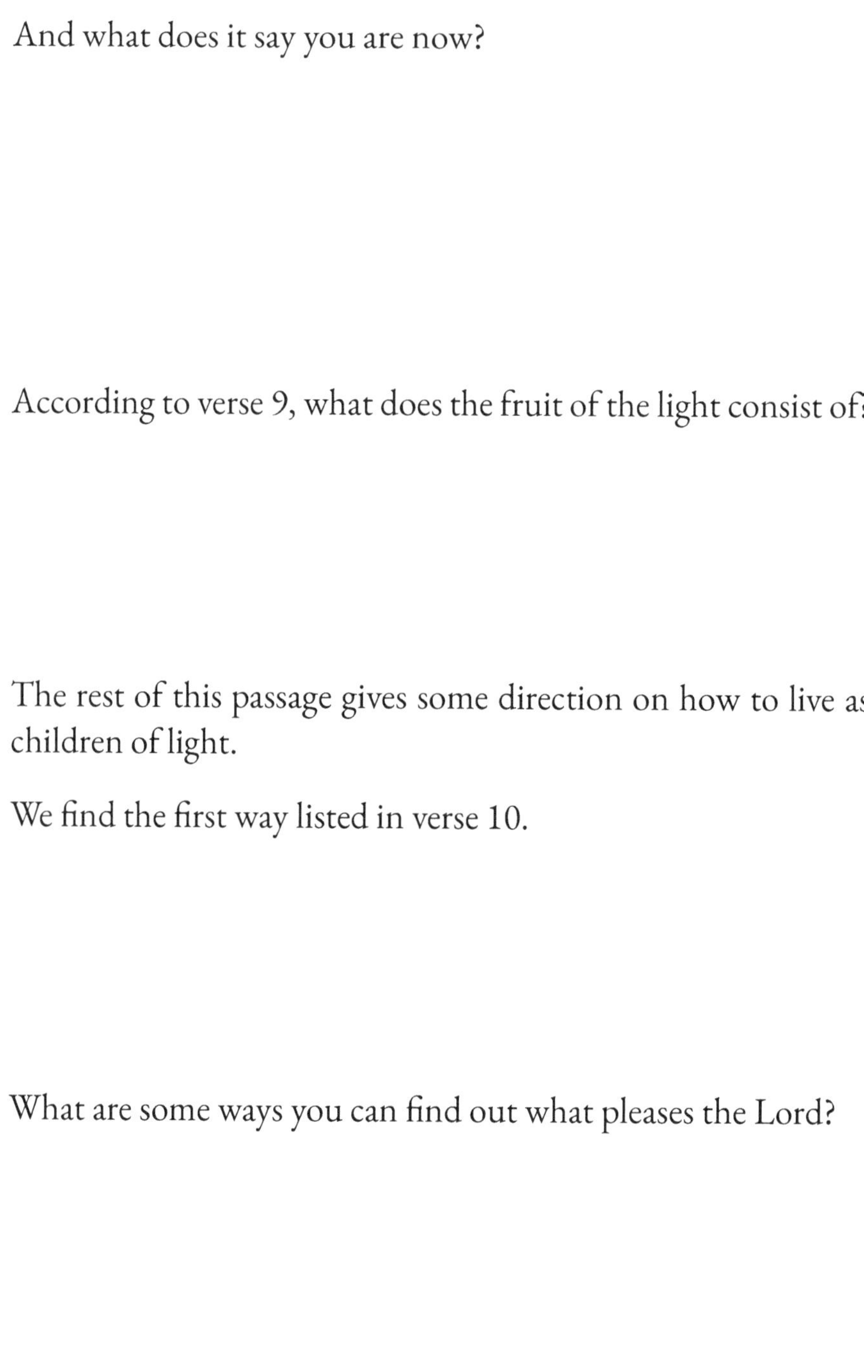

And what does it say you are now?

According to verse 9, what does the fruit of the light consist of?

The rest of this passage gives some direction on how to live as children of light.

We find the first way listed in verse 10.

What are some ways you can find out what pleases the Lord?

Another way to live as children of light is in verse 11. What are we to have nothing to do with?

Tool

The tool we are going to pick up today is telling Jesus we want to live a fruitful life and asking for His help in putting that into practice. I invite you to pray the following prayer with me. Read the prayer silently to yourself, and if it resonates with you, pray it out loud from your heart to God.

> Father God, I want to live a fruitful life for You. I surrender my life to You, and I ask that You help me to follow Your wisdom, living by Your leading that I find in Your Word and prayer. I pray that as I live for You, that Your presence will become more real in my life, and that I would sense You with me every step of the way, pouring out Your wisdom so that I can live a life that is fruitful for Your Kingdom. Lord, I give to You any place in my life that has been fruitless, and I ask that You help me to become fruitful in all areas of my life. In Jesus' mighty name, amen.

Walk It Out In Everyday Life

Each day, spend a little bit of time with Jesus, asking Him to direct your steps and give you wisdom for the day. Know that those small steps in following Him lead to the biggest victories.

More Instruction

Read Ephesians 5:15-20

“Application! Application! Application!” Our teacher’s voice boomed across the room.

It was the start of our First John class in Bible college, and the teacher was trying to make his point early on.

Through the entire quarter of studying First John as a class, the application of the Word was drilled into our hearts and minds. We were not just to *read* the Word, but we were to walk it out in everyday life.

That is what walking in the light means (See 1 John 1:7), reading the Word and applying it to your own life and situation.

Today, we are going to pick up the tool of application, choosing one thing from the Word to start walking out in our daily lives.

Reflect

This passage starts out with, “Be very careful, then, how you live,” (NIV) and then gives some pointers on things *to do*, and things *not to do*.

Verse 17 has one do not, and one do. Write each in the space provided.

Do not:

Do:

Verse 18 has one do not, and one do.

Do not:

Do:

Verse 19 tells you how you can be filled with the Spirit.

What two things does verse 19 tell you to do?

Do:

Do:

We move on to verse 20, which tells us to do one thing:

Do:

Tool

The tool we are going to pick up today is applying the Word to our own lives and situations. Out of all these dos and don'ts, which one spoke to your heart the most?

How can you put one of these into practice in your life this week?

Say a prayer to your Father in Heaven asking Him to help you walk out this truth in your life. Without Him and His help we can do nothing (See John 15:4-5).

Walk It Out In Everyday Life

When you read the Word, and especially when something you read stands out to you, think about how that verse or passage applies to your life and situation.

Wounded

Read Ephesians 5:21-24

All Scripture is God breathed and meant for good, but sometimes, fallen people have used Scripture to hurt and wound others.

There are a couple of them that bring up some bad memories for me. I won't say what Scriptures they are, but people who were trying to manipulate me used them to try and guilt me out of setting boundaries.

When you experience hurt in your life, it's painful already. But to experience hurt from anyone who claims to live for Christ and uses the Word of God to manipulate you or justify their behavior, can be unbearable.

Please know that God does not want you to stay in a place where you are being mentally or physically abused. This verse is talking about a *healthy* relationship, about a husband loving his wife as Christ loved the Church (See Ephesians 5:25).

Today, we will reflect on this passage, what it means to submit in a *healthy* relationship, and reflect on any abuse of the Word we may have experienced in our lives.

Reflect

What emotions does the passage for today bring up in you?

If you are married and in a healthy relationship, what is one instance where you submitted to your husband as to the Lord?

How did this situation turn out?

Is there a time that you didn't, and wanted to go your own way?

How did that situation turn out?

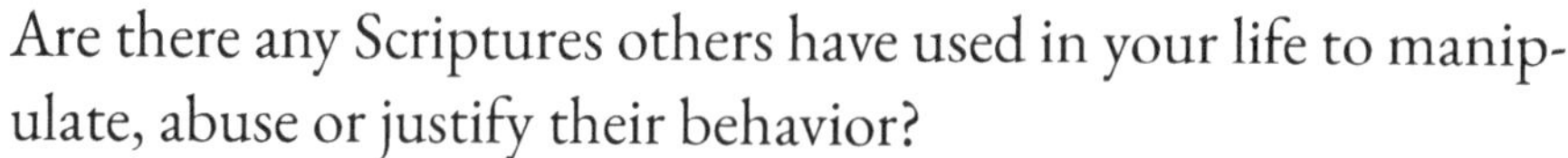

Are there any Scriptures others have used in your life to manipulate, abuse or justify their behavior?

How do you feel when you hear those Scriptures now?

Tool

The tool we will pick up again today is asking God to heal us where we have been wounded. Read the following prayer silently to yourself, and if it resonates with you, read it out loud from your heart to God.

> Father God, I surrender to you the places in my heart and life where Your truth that was meant to bring life was yielded for evil instead. I choose to forgive those who wielded Your Scripture with evil intent, and I ask for Your healing for my heart, soul, mind,

and emotions. I pray over any relationships in my life that have been affected because of this and ask that You bring these relationships into alignment with You and Your ways. Lord, where I have seen authority figures to be controlling, manipulative and hurtful, heal the places in my soul where I have seen You like that. Bring healing, wholeness, and a knowledge of who You truly are, a good and awesome God, who feels compassion, kindness, and love toward me. In Jesus' mighty name, amen.

Walk It Out In Everyday Life

When you hear a Scripture that you find yourself having an adverse reaction to, ask the Lord what's at the root of that reaction? Then, trust Him to show you. Remember that the Lord does not leave you alone to heal, but walks with you, never abandons you, and keeps His Word. In Jesus' name, amen.

Freedom From Shame

Read Ephesians 5:25-33

I was at a Cleansing Stream retreat for the very first time, and the topic they were praying about was shame.

As they taught the topic, I felt this well of emotions rise up within me. I knew I had struggled with *something*, but I hadn't realized it was shame.

When they called people up for prayer, I wanted to run instead of walk. And when I stood in front of a person who was ready to pray for me, the sobs came, shaking my whole body, and I couldn't even speak.

It was like God was washing that shame, that condemnation and judgement right from the inside of me.

I had accepted Christ, but I hadn't received the truth that God cleansed me.

That day was the beginning of a whole new journey for me. A journey of realizing I was not only given eternal life, but I was given healing from the shame I felt from a past that I had tried to hide from.

Jesus didn't want me hiding anymore.

At the end of our prayer time, the person praying for me asked me to look up to Heaven and let God look upon me. And for the first time, I felt like I didn't have to try to hide, I could open my heart to Him and not be afraid of judgement or condemnation.

If you have struggled with any type of shame, I pray that this chapter helps you to heal.

Reflect

As you read the following verses, write down what each verse says Christ did for you. I would even suggest you put your name in the place of what Christ did for the church. Remember, you are a part of the church, Christ's own body.

25.

26.

27.

29.

Lastly, what does verse 30 say you are?

Tool

The tool we are revisiting today is asking the Lord for healing. This tool is so important, because we cannot walk in freedom without God's help.

If you struggle with shame, as I did, read the following prayer silently to yourself. If it resonates with you, pray it out loud from your heart to God.

> Father God, I surrender to You the shame I have felt about myself and situations in my life. I break the power of shame off me now and renounce every agreement I have made with shame. In the name of Jesus, shame, I tell you to leave me now. I will give you no more room in my life. I take the spiritual garments of shame off, and I receive the garment of praise, the garment of love and the garment of Jesus Christ as my Savior. I pray Father God, that You would heal me of all shame, and show me that I am loved, forgiven and that I don't have to hide from You. Help me to know that when You look at me,

you see the righteousness of Jesus Christ. In Jesus' mighty name, Amen.

Walk It Out In Everyday Life

Take these truths you have written out, with your name in them, and put them in a short paragraph of what Christ has done for you. Place this in a spot where you can see it regularly and read it out loud for the next 30 days.

Serving the Lord

Read Ephesians 6:1-9

Lately, I've been learning about how my role as a mother changes when my children become adults. They're both in their twenties at this writing, and I have done my very best to raise them up in the Lord.

But then, the letting go must happen.

They are not my little babies to train up anymore; they are young adults, making their own decisions and beginning to lead their own lives.

In this transition, I've learned that giving advice without it being asked for is usually taken as criticism, and that my children want me in their lives, but they don't want to be told what to do anymore.

They must make their own mistakes and learn from them.

Sometimes, I watch with fear, praying that God will cover them, and other times, I am so proud of the decisions they are making and the people they have become.

As adults, to honor your father and mother doesn't mean you always do what they want or let them control you. It means taking the good they have taught you and doing the most with it, living your life for the audience of One, Father God, and being thankful for the good things that were given to you.

Reflect

In the following passages, name who Paul is talking to:

Verses 1-3:

Verse 4:

Verse 5:

Verse 9:

This passage speaks of the first command with a promise. What is it?

What is the command from verse 7?

And what is the promise in verse 8?

Do any of these verses speak to your heart?

Tool

The tool we are going to pick up today is realizing that whatever we do, we are to do it unto the Lord, and not for people.

Is there any place in your life where you have done things for the approval of people, or to please them, instead of following your own heart?

If you have, I invite you to pray the following prayer with me. Read it silently to yourself, and if it resonates with you, pray it out loud from your heart to God.

Father God, in the name of Jesus, I ask Your forgiveness for any place I have put pleasing people over and above pleasing You, or following what You have placed on my heart. Help me, Lord, to honor those who have sowed into my life, but also not allow myself to be manipulated or controlled. Help me Father, to serve You with my whole heart in everything I do, everything I give, and in every relationship You've placed in my life. In Jesus' mighty name, amen.

Walk It Out In Everyday Life

Whenever you feel pressure from people, stop and pray, asking God to help you follow *His* heart and *His* will for your life; that you would honor, yes, but not allow yourself to be manipulated or controlled.

Be Strong in the Lord

Read Ephesians 6:10-13

"You seem stronger somehow." My friend commented.

She didn't know it, but that very week, I had felt the Lord's nudge to start memorizing Scripture. And I'd started to memorize Scriptures that spoke to my heart about my current situation.

Her words were confirmation that I was doing the right thing.

I had found myself in a series of spiritual battles that tested my faith. I'm certain that the only way I made it without falling apart was through the Word and prayer.

That time in prayer and worship is when I felt led to memorize Scripture. Although I didn't fully realize it, it was like God was telling me to pick up my sword, which is the Word, and begin to fight with it.

Today we are going to talk about how we can become strong in the Lord and learn more about our primary weapon in battle, the Word of God.

Reflect

What does verse 10 say we are to be strong in?

By Whose power do we do this?

Who does verse 12 say our struggle is really against?

Whether you like it or not, you will find yourself in spiritual battles when you live on this earth. Many stories are written about the war between good and evil, but there is a war going on in the spirit realms even now.

What battle are you fighting right now?

According to the Word, who is your battle against?

Look up 2 Timothy 2:26.

What does this say to you about some people being held captive to do the enemy's will?

Look up 2 Corinthians 10:3-4.

What do these verses say about how we are to wage war as Christians?

Tomorrow we will talk more about the armor of God, but right now I want you to know that one of our primary weapons we fight with is the Word of God.

We Declare it.

We Pray it.

We memorize it.

We tear down strongholds and we take captive the negative thoughts with the Word of God.

Look up Hebrews 4:12.

What does this verse say the Word is?

After reading who our battle is against, how we are to war as Christians and learning more about what our primary weapon is, is the Lord speaking to your heart about anything in particular?

Tool

The tool we are going to pick up today is to pray the Word back to God.

When you come across a verse or passage that speaks to your current situation, encourages you or gives you strength, turn that verse into a prayer.

For example, If I were to pray Isaiah 55:11 which says.

"So is my word that goes out from my mouth: It will not return to me empty, but will accomplish what I desire and achieve the purpose for which I sent it," (NIV).

I could start by praying,

Thank you, Father God, that Your Word will not return to You empty, that it will accomplish Your will, and achieve Your Purposes.

Then, I could add my own prayer to the rest of that which might be something like:

I pray, Father God, that Your will would be done, and Your Kingdom would come in this situation I am walking through. Strengthen me by Your Word, by Your Spirit and by Your power. In Jesus' mighty name, amen.

Walk It Out In Everyday Life

When you read the Word, ask the Lord to strengthen and encourage you through His Word, and when you come across verses that give you strength, memorize those verses and pray them back to God.

The Armor

Read Ephesians 6:14-17

When training for ministry, especially before retreats where we spent the day praying with people for spiritual healing and deliverance, we always prayed and put on our armor. I'll share a prayer with you today, to put on your own armor, but I also wanted to talk about what I found as I studied the passage for today.

The armor that we are to put on is supposed to help us stand firm in the battle with the enemy, and that armor is listed in this passage. What I noticed is this armor begins and ends with the Word of God.

First, we are to put on the belt of truth, and the truth begins with the Word. The last part of the Armor is the Sword of the Spirit, which is the Word of God.

Our armor, our defense from the enemy, our strength to stand, all begins and ends with having the Word of God in our hearts and minds. It will help us combat the lies of the enemy and stand in the truth of who God says we are.

No matter where you are in this world, you are a light, shining in the darkness, and putting on this armor will help you stand in the face of battle. That armor begins and ends with the Word of God.

Reflect

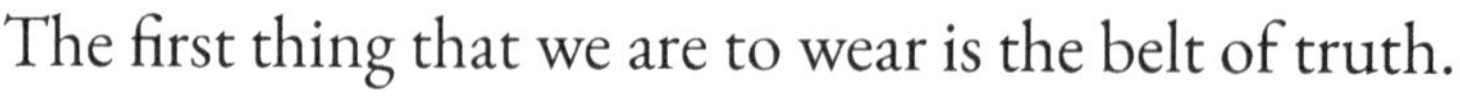
The first thing that we are to wear is the belt of truth.

Look up John 8:31-32.

What does Jesus say we are to abide or continue in?

And when you abide or continue in it, you shall know what?

And it will make you free.

The second thing we are to put on is the Breastplate of righteousness.

Look up 2 Corinthians 5:21.

What does this verse speak to your heart about Jesus' gift of righteousness to you?

The Third thing we are to put on is the shoes of the Gospel of peace.

Look up 2 Corinthians 5:18-19 and Romans 5:1.

Through Jesus' death and resurrection on the cross, what did God do for us?

And what do we have with Him?

The fourth piece of armor we are to take up is the shield of faith.

Look up Jude 1:20.

Look up Matthew 17:20.

Even if you have faith that is the smallest seed, you still have faith, dear sister, and you can build that faith by abiding, and continuing in the Word of God, and by praying in the Holy Spirit. Don't ever think of yourself as weak because Christ lives in you, and He will help you, lead you, and guide you.

You may be in a battle, but Christ, who has overcome the world (See John 16:33) is with you in it and will never leave you nor forsake you (See Hebrews 13:5).

The next piece of armor is our helmet of salvation, the surety that we are saved by His grace.

Take a quick look at Ephesians 2:8-9 and remind yourself of what these verses say about salvation being a gift from God, not of your own works.

And finally, we are to take up the Sword of the Spirit, which is the Word of God.

Look up 2 Timothy 2:15.

We can grow in our knowledge of the Word no matter what season of life we are in. No matter how much time you have, small or great amounts, you can do *something* to grow just a little, each day or each week, by spending time with Jesus in the Word.

Tool

I invite you to pray with me today, putting on our armor spiritually.

> In the name of Jesus, I put on my belt of truth, my breastplate of righteousness, and my shoes of the Gospel of peace. I take up my shield of faith, my helmet of salvation, and my sword of the Spirit, which is the Word of God. And Father God, I pray, that as I read the Word, that You would do a work in me, speak to my heart about the situations I am in, and fill me with wisdom by Your Word and by Your Holy Spirit, in Jesus' mighty name, amen.

Walk It Out In Everyday Life

Today, I want you to think about some of the tools that we've been learning about in this study. Which one is your favorite? How has it impacted you as you've used it in everyday life?

Prayer

Read Ephesians 6:18-23

We've just put on our spiritual armor, which begins and ends with the Word of God. But notice, as you read verse 17 and move on to verse 18, that the sentence doesn't end there.

There is another piece to this, not often talked about with the rest.

And that is prayer.

Prayer also is a powerful weapon against the enemy, and when you pray, things are happening in the spirit realm that you cannot see in the natural world. If things in your life are not moving and you've prayed, keep on praying and don't give up, for prayer is a powerful weapon!

Reflect

Today, we're going to start out by looking at Daniel 10:12-13.

What does this passage say was happening in the spirit realm while Daniel prayed?

We are also going to look at Psalm 66:20. What does David say about his prayer in this Psalm?

When you pray, and you don't see anything right away, know that there is something happening in the spirit realm, even if you don't see it.

The enemy may pelt your mind with thoughts when you pray, that it isn't working, that you're wasting your time, or any other thing he can say to get you to stop praying.

What does Ephesians 6:18 instruct us about prayer?

Tool

Today, the tool we are going to pick up is practicing prayer in our daily lives.

Remember that everyone is in a different season of life. Some have more time than others. Being aware of the season of life you are in, without comparing yourself to others, what is one way you can put prayer into practice if you haven't already done so?

Walk It Out In Everyday Life

When you've been praying for something and don't see anything in the natural world, or things even get worse, remember that there are things going on in the spiritual realm that you don't see. Remind yourself that your prayers are making a difference and are a powerful weapon against the enemy.

About the Author

Carolyn Rice holds an Associate Degree in Biblical studies and has worked in several aspects of ministry, including teaching Cleansing Stream Seminars, and serving as the Alumni Director for Seattle Bible College. Carolyn hosts the Abide in Jesus podcast and has written several books on finding healing in Christ. She is a survivor of abuse and wants to share the healing she found in Jesus with others.

She has two grown children, one granddaughter, and lives with her husband and two dogs in Granite Falls, Washington.

Find out more about Carolyn and her books at

CarolynsBooks.com

Also By Carolyn Rice

Lord, Heal My Heart: A Devotional

Lord, Help Me Forgive: An 8-Week Journey through Forgiveness

Loved by the Father: A Women's Bible Study through John and First John

Healing the Father Wound: A Women's Bible Study through the Gospel of Mark

Listen to the the podcast, Abide in Jesus, wherever you download podcasts.

This Page Intentionally Left Blank

www.ingramcontent.com/pod-product-compliance
Ingram Content Group UK Ltd.
Pitfield, Milton Keynes, MK11 3LW, UK
UKHW021934200726
13853UKWH00011B/2025

9 798986 967912